D0792200

NS ALIVE

# Lobsters

by **Martha E. H. Rustad**

BLASTOFF!
2
READERS

BELLWETHER MEDIA · MINNEAPOLIS, MN

Note to Librarians, Teachers, and Parents:

**Blastoff! Readers** are carefully developed by literacy experts and combine standards-based content with developmentally-appropriate text.

**Level 1** provides the most support through repetition of high-frequency words, light text, predictable sentence patterns, and strong visual support.

**Level 2** offers early readers a bit more challenge through varied simple sentences, increased text load, and less repetition of high frequency words.

**Level 3** advances early-fluent readers toward fluency through increased text and concept load, less reliance on visuals, longer sentences, and more literary language.

**Level 4** builds reading stamina by providing more text per page, increased use of punctuation, greater variation in sentence patterns, and increasingly challenging vocabulary.

**Level 5** encourages children to move from "learning to read" to "reading to learn" by providing even more text, varied writing styles, and less familiar topics.

Whichever book is right for your reader, Blastoff! Readers are the perfect books to build confidence and encourage a love of reading that will last a lifetime!

This edition first published in 2008 by Bellwether Media.

No part of this publication may be reproduced in whole or in part without written permission of the publisher. For information regarding permission, write to Bellwether Media Inc., Attention: Permissions Department, Post Office Box 1C, Minnetonka, MN 55345-9998.

Library of Congress Cataloging-in-Publication Data
Rustad, Martha E. H. (Martha Elizabeth Hillman), 1975–
    Lobsters / by Martha E. H. Rustad.
       p. cm. (Blastoff! readers. Oceans alive)
Summary: "Simple text and supportive images introduce beginning readers to lobsters. Intended for students in kindergarten through third grade"—Provided by publisher.
    Includes bibliographical references and index.
    ISBN-13: 978-1-60014-082-2 (hardcover : alk. paper)
    ISBN-10: 1-60014-082-3 (hardcover : alk. paper)
    1. Lobsters—Juvenile literature. I. Title.

QL444.M33R87 2008
595.3'84—dc22                                    2007009795

# Contents

Lobsters are ocean animals
with a shell on the outside
of their bodies.

The shell is their **skeleton**.

Lobsters come in many different colors.

A lobster's shell cannot grow.
A lobster must **shed** its shell
and grow a new one.

Lobsters eat small ocean animals such as crabs, clams, and fish.

Lobsters walk along the
ocean floor at night in
search of food.

9

Lobsters have ten legs.
They use the eight back
legs to walk.

10

The front legs have claws called **pincers**. They use pincers to catch food.

Pincers also help lobsters eat.
Their strong grip can crush the
hard shells of crabs or clams.

12

Pincers rip food into small
pieces the lobster can eat.

Lobsters have four **antennas**.
Tiny hairs cover the antennas.

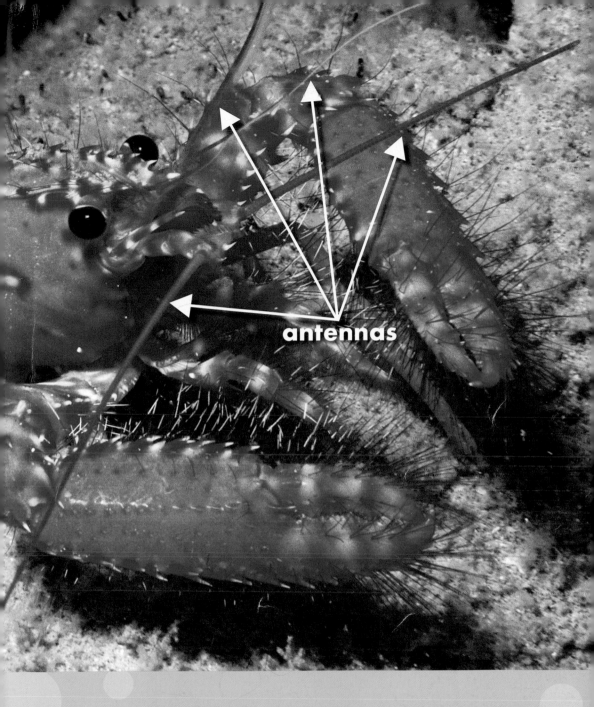

antennas

Lobsters flick their antennas to smell.

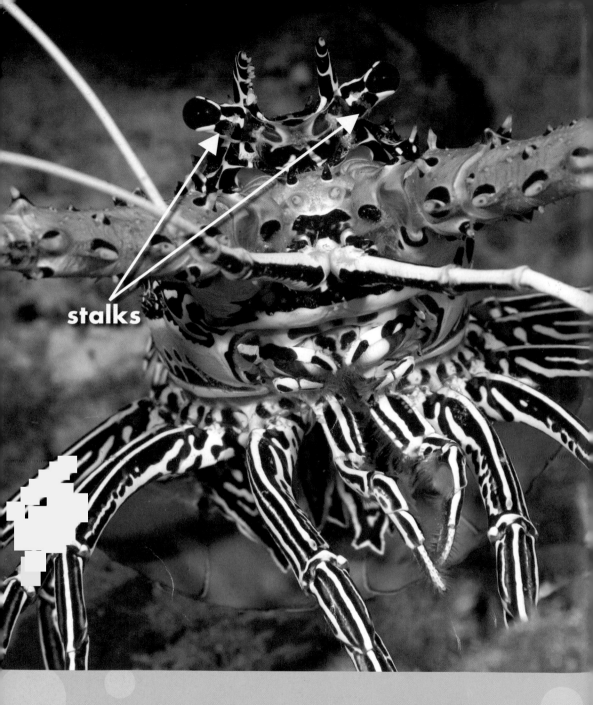

stalks

Lobsters have eyes on **stalks**.

Lobsters watch out for big fish or other ocean animals that might try to eat them.

Lobsters curl and uncurl
their bodies to move
backward quickly.

This helps them move into a
hiding place.

Lobsters hide in sand
or rocks during the day.

They catch small ocean animals that pass by their hiding place. Surprise!

# Glossary

**antennas**—long and thin feelers on an animal's head

**pincer**—a front claw

**shed**—to take off

**skeleton**—the hard structure that supports the body of an animal

**stalks**—a long, thin structure

# To Learn More

**AT THE LIBRARY**
Gordon, Sharon. *Guess Who Snaps*. New York:
Benchmark Books, 2005.

Hirschmann, Kris. *Lobsters*. Detroit, Mich.: KidHaven
Press, 2005.

Rake, Jody Sullivan. *Lobsters*. Mankato, Minn.:
Capstone Press, 2007.

Schaefer, Lola. *Lobsters*. Chicago, Ill.: Heinemann
Library, 2002.

**ON THE WEB**
Learning more about lobsters
is as easy as 1, 2, 3.

1. Go to www.factsurfer.com

2. Enter "lobsters" into search box.

3. Click the "Surf" button and you will see a list of
   related web sites.

With factsurfer.com, finding more information is just a
click away.

# Index

The photographs in this book are reproduced through the courtesy of: mpemberton, front cover; Nick Caloyianis/Getty Images, pp. 4-5; Roger Steene/imagequestmarine.com, pp. 6-7, 18-19; Brian J. Skerry/Getty Images, pp. 8-9, 17; Chris A. Crumley/Alamy, p. 10; Geoff Brightling/Getty, p 11; Marevision/Age fotostock, pp. 12, 20; Reinhard Dirscherl/Age fotostock, p. 13; Chris Newbert/Minden Pictures, pp. 14-15 ; David Fleetham/Alamy, pp. 16, 21.